BBC Children's Books
Published by the Penguin Group
Penguin Books Ltd, 80 Strand, London, WC2R 0RL, England
Penguin Group (Australia) Ltd, 250 Camberwell Road, Camberwell,
Victoria 3124, Australia (a division of Pearson Australia Group Pty Ltd)
Canada, India, New Zealand, South Africa

Published by BBC Children's Books, 2011
Text and design © Children's Character Books, 2011

002 - 10 9 8 7 6 5 4 3 2

Written by Sam Philip
Designed by Dan Newman, Perfect Bound Ltd

ISBN: 9781405907934

Printed in China

Thanks to the following photographers for the use
of their images: Rod Barker /Jeremy Davey/Mike
Hearn (Thrust SSC, © SSC Programme Ltd),
David Cooper/dazecoop.com (Chaparral 2F), digital
leica (Citroën DS), Andy Dingley (Babs), Don
France (Benetton B186 F1 car), ignis (Trabant),
Sébastien Morliere (Italdesign Aztec), Parajet
Automotive (Parajet Skycar) Oliver Payan (Citroën
2CV Sahara), Jordi Roqué (Babs), Lothar Spurzem
(Chaparral 2F), Rudolf Stricker (Citroën DS),
Tim Whittington/RallycrossUK.com (Rover Metro
6R4 rally car).

Contents

Introduction

A mad car is made up of more than numbers. Horsepower, acceleration, top speed – yes, they're all part of the recipe, but there's something else that sets a truly bonkers machine apart from the regular, sensible stuff on the roads. Maybe it's the smell of burning oil wafting gently from under its bonnet. Maybe it's the telltale signs of an engine that's too big and too powerful, spilling out of the car like a sleeping bag from a stuff sack. Maybe it's the knowledge that, given the chance, it'll fling you from the driver's seat and into the next county.

But, like the mysterious composition of the Stig himself, no one knows exactly what makes a truly mad car. All we know is that the hundred cars squeezed into this book are the maddest, baddest, looniest vehicles ever to be cooked up in factories, garages and sheds around the world. Some of them are seriously fast. Some of them are seriously expensive. Some are cheap and slow and frankly a bit rubbish. But all of them will leave you wondering what on earth was going on in the brains of the men and women who created these fearsome concoctions. The truth is... no one knows.

The Stigometer
If anyone was ever qualified to judge the madness of a car, it's *Top Gear*'s white-suited racing driver. And beware: cars that score a maximum five Stig helmets aren't to be trusted. They're as mad as a grizzly bear who's lost his wallet...

DeLorean
DMC-12

01

The DeLorean DMC-12 is most famous for its starring role as the time travelling car in the *Back to the Future* films. The real DMC-12 couldn't time travel – in fact, it wasn't much cop at standard road travel – but it was bonkers all the same. First built in Northern Ireland in 1981, it sported huge gull wing doors, futuristic angular styling... and not very much speed at all.

Though it looked fast enough to hop at light-speed between centuries, the DMC-12, with its 2.8-litre V6, took more than ten seconds to hit 60mph! It was a financial flop, and the DeLorean Motor Company collapsed within a year. The DMC-12 might have become entirely forgotten if it wasn't for one Marty McFly...

 Power: 156bhp

 0-60mph: 10.5 seconds

 Top speed: 140mph

 Price: £10,000

 Mad rating:

Lamborghini builds some of the maddest supercars on the planet, but they're not much good if you need to transport more than two people. You could probably squeeze four into a Murcielago, but the two passengers wedged in the glovebox won't be very impressed. What you need is an Estoque – Lamborghini's four-door, four-seat rival to the Porsche Panamera and Aston Martin Rapide, but far, far madder than both. There's just one tiny problem: the Estoque only exists as a concept at the moment. However, Lamborghini says it might bring it to the road in the next few years. Keep your fingers crossed!

Power: 500bhp

0-60mph: About 4 seconds

Top speed: 200mph approx

Price: At least £200,000

Mad rating:

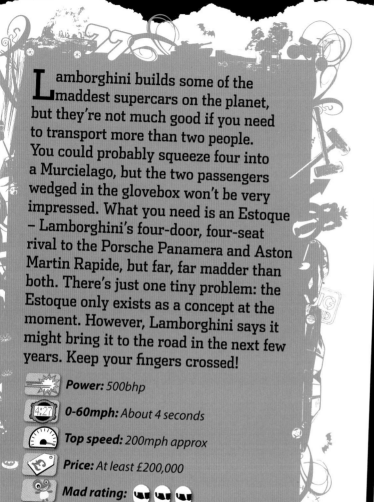

Lamborghini
Estoque concept

02

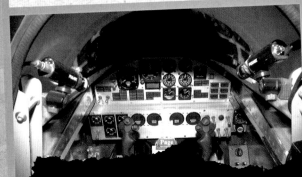

Thrust SSC

03

The Thrust SSC is the fastest car in history. In 1997, the British car clocked an amazing 763mph in the Black Rock Desert in America, with British pilot Andy Green at the controls. It was the first car ever to travel faster than the speed of sound, causing a sonic boom as it passed what fighter pilots call 'Mach 1'.

And before you say anything – yes, it **is** a car. It has wheels. And, er, a pair of huge jet engines producing 110,000bhp. At full speed, Thrust SSC burned four gallons of fuel **every second!**

Will anything ever beat its record? Well, the Thrust team are building an even faster car – called Bloodhound – which they say could break 1000mph in the next couple of years...

Power: *110,000bhp*

0-60mph: *35 seconds – really!*

Top speed: *763mph*

Price: *Over £15,000,000*

Mad rating:

Back in the 1950s, when scientists predicted what humans would be driving in the year 2000 and beyond, they always drew up a low, sleek supercar with a bubble-shaped roof. Of course, we aren't really driving cars like that nowadays. We're driving Ford Focuses. And Toyota Priuses.

But the Maserati Birdcage, a concept shown at the Geneva motor show in 2005, was the car those poor 1950s scientists always wanted. Powered by the V12 engine from the Ferrari Enzo, it produced a screaming 700bhp and could get to 60mph in fewer than three seconds. But the Birdcage's best trick came when it was time for the driver to get out. The entire windscreen and roof hinged up and away from the rest of the car, like the cockpit of a jet fighter...

 Power: *700bhp*

 0-60mph: *Fewer than 3 seconds*

 Top speed: *More than 200mph*

 Price: *N/A*

 Mad rating:

Maserati
Birdcage

04

15

The Pikes Peak hill climb is one of the most dangerous races in the world: a 12.4 mile track that climbs almost a mile to the peak of one of America's scariest mountains, with thousand-foot cliffs beckoning at the sides. The top of Pikes Peak is so high that there's barely enough oxygen to breathe!

Unlike Formula 1 or WRC, there are no restrictions at all on the cars or engines that can race up the hill: the only aim is to be the quickest car to the top. The four-wheel drive Suzuki XL7 is the fastest race car to conquer Pikes Peak. In 2007, Japanese racing driver Nobuhiro Tajima completed the hill climb in ten minutes and one second in the insane four-wheel drive. However, he's vowed to break the ten minute barrier in the next few years!

Power: *995bhp*

0-60mph: *3 seconds on dirt*

Top speed: *140mph*

Price: *Millions!*

Mad rating:

Suzuki
XL7

05

Tyrrell
P34

06

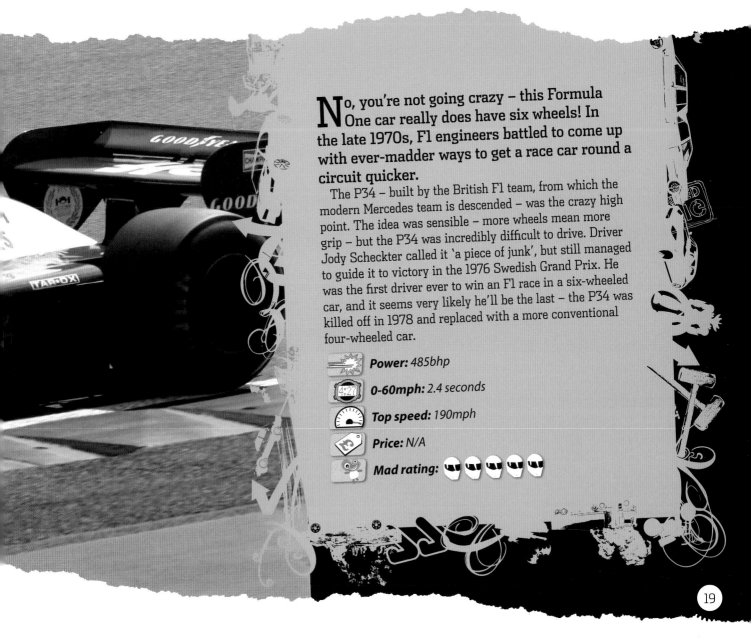

No, you're not going crazy – this Formula One car really does have six wheels! In the late 1970s, F1 engineers battled to come up with ever-madder ways to get a race car round a circuit quicker.

The P34 – built by the British F1 team, from which the modern Mercedes team is descended – was the crazy high point. The idea was sensible – more wheels mean more grip – but the P34 was incredibly difficult to drive. Driver Jody Scheckter called it 'a piece of junk', but still managed to guide it to victory in the 1976 Swedish Grand Prix. He was the first driver ever to win an F1 race in a six-wheeled car, and it seems very likely he'll be the last – the P34 was killed off in 1978 and replaced with a more conventional four-wheeled car.

Power: *485bhp*

0-60mph: *2.4 seconds*

Top speed: *190mph*

Price: *N/A*

Mad rating:

The Smart ForTwo is a very sensible car if you live in the middle of a busy city: the two-seaters are so tiny that you can fit a pair of them into a standard parking space. However, it's not a very mad car.

Unless, that is, you bolt one to the wheels of a Mercedes Unimog. Standing 3.7 metres high – or taller than one large man standing on another's shoulders – the ForFun2 is powered by a mammoth diesel engine nearly ten times the size of the motor in the normal Smart ForTwo. Each of those monster truck wheels measures 140cm across, giving the sensible little Smart the ability to scale sand dunes and cliffs with ease. Don't worry that it won't fit in a city parking space: you can just park on top of everything else!

 Power: *84bhp*

 0-60mph: *Never!*

 Top speed: *55mph*

 Price: *N/A*

 Mad rating:

Smart
ForFun2

07

Rinspeed

Splash

08

Plenty of bonkers inventors have built cars that can float on water. Even Jeremy, James and Richard managed it... with a bit of practice! But what about a car that doesn't just float on water, but skims over the top of it?

That sort of thinking requires the bonkers boffins at Swiss company Rinspeed. When you've reached the limits of dry land in the Splash, just drive into the water and engage the 'hydrofoil' – a series of blades that drop into the water – and fire up the propeller. Magically, the Splash will rise above the sea as it accelerates to 50mph on water. That's fast enough to tow a waterskier behind!

Power: *140bhp*

0-60mph: *5.9 seconds*

Top speed: *124mph approx*

Price: *Not for sale!*

Mad rating:

Yes, the Lotus Carlton looks like a sensible family car from the early 1990s. That's because it was and that's exactly why it was so mad!

The Vauxhall Carlton was last century's equivalent of the Ford Mondeo – a dull, grown-up car driven by dull grown-up people. Until the engineers at Lotus got their hands on it. They left the exterior almost unchanged, but fitted a bigger engine with two turbochargers and a whole load of shiny racing bits to create the world's fastest, most understated four-door saloon car. The Carlton's maddest statistic was that it could race from a standing start to 100mph, then brake to a complete halt in fewer than fifteen seconds. That's neck-snapping stuff!

Lotus Carlton

09

Power: 377bhp

0-60mph: 5.2 seconds

Top speed: 175mph

Price: £48,000

Mad rating: ●●●

There are mad concepts... and then there's the Cadillac Sixteen. Built by Cadillac – the American company better known for big soggy luxury cars – in 2003, it packed one of the scariest engines in history: a 13.6-litre monster with sixteen cylinders!

It produced more than 1000bhp, the same as a Bugatti Veyron, but the Veyron uses turbochargers to reach its monster power output. The Sixteen didn't have a turbo or supercharger in sight: it was naturally aspirated, just like a Formula One car. And, unlike the safe, four-wheel drive Veyron, it was rear-wheel drive. Maybe it was best for public safety that it never made it to production. Oh, and Cadillac didn't entirely forget that they're best known for building luxury cars: in the middle of the Sixteen's steering wheel was a Cadillac logo... carved from solid crystal!

Power: *More than 1000bhp*

0-60mph: *2.5 seconds*

Top speed: *253mph*

Price: *N/A*

Mad rating: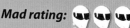

Cadillac
Sixteen

10

Gibbs
Aquada

11

Richard Branson, the billionaire owner of Virgin, isn't a man to do things by halves. So when in 2004, he decided to break the record for crossing the English Channel in an amphibious car – which had stood at six hours for over forty years – he needed a serious piece of machinery.

The Gibbs Aquada is a serious piece of machinery. It'll do 100mph on dry land thanks to a V6 engine, and 30mph on water thanks to a jet, its wheels tucking neatly under its body. Did Branson

break the record? Of course he did. Wearing a tuxedo, he crossed from England to France in one hour and forty minutes, shaving more than four hours off the previous best time!

Power: *175bhp*

0-60mph: *9.0 seconds*

Top speed: *100mph*

Price: *£150,000*

Mad rating: 🚗🚗🚗🚗

Some cars are built of steel. Some are built of aluminium. Some are built of fibreglass. But only the BMW Gina is built of lycra – the material used to make leotards and cycle suits!

With a 'skeleton' of wires under its stretchy skin, Gina can shift shape at the driver's command, growing a rear spoiler or bigger wheel arches as the wires push outwards. Gina can even 'wink', as the fabric skin closes down over the headlights. And, because it's made of stretchy material rather than metal, it'll never rust. Just make sure you don't get too close to it if you're carrying a pair of scissors!

Power: *500bhp*

0-60mph: *4 seconds*

Top speed: *N/A*

Price: *N/A*

Mad rating: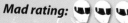

12

BMW Gina

concept

Tango
T600

13

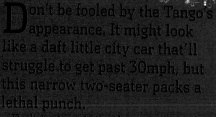

Don't be fooled by the Tango's appearance. It might look like a daft little city car that'll struggle to get past 30mph, but this narrow two-seater packs a lethal punch.

Built in America and running on electric power alone, it can get to 60mph in fewer than four seconds and won't stop accelerating until it reaches 150mph! The Tango measures less than a metre across, meaning two of them will squeeze into a single motorway lane. The first ever Tango T600 was bought by Hollywood actor, George Clooney, but its £70,000 price tag means Tango ownership might be limited to celebrities!

 Power: 805bhp.

 0-60mph: 3.9 seconds.

 Top speed: More than 150 mph.

 Price: £70,000.

 Mad rating:

BMW Vision

concept

14

Ever wondered what supercars will look like in the future? According to BMW, they'll look something like the amazing Vision Efficient Dynamics concept.

The glassy, layered body is tricky enough to understand, but its combination of motors is even more complicated! The Vision concept has a tiny diesel engine and a pair of electric motors, which might sound a bit sensible but will fire the four-seater to 60mph in under five seconds. It'll also do seventy-five miles per gallon, meaning you won't have to stop at the petrol station every two hours to refill the tank. Fast **and** cheap to run – the future sounds bright!

 Power: *350bhp*

 0-60mph: *4.8 seconds*

 Top speed: *150mph*

 Price: *N/A*

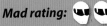 **Mad rating:**

Brabus Bullitt

The Mercedes-Benz C-Class is a sensible car. The sort of car that might be driven by an accountant. Or a lawyer. Until the crazy German tuners at Brabus get their hands on it, that is.

Somehow they've managed to squeeze a 6.3-litre twin-turbo V12 engine into the front of the small, sensible C-Class, a giant engine producing 720bhp. That's like wedging a nuclear bomb into a shoe! The result is one of the slidiest, scariest, fastest four-door cars ever created, a car that can accelerate from a standing start to 124mph in just ten seconds. Who on earth could tame a car like this? Sounds like a job for one white-suited racing driver...

 Power: 720bhp

 0-60mph: 3.8 seconds

 Top speed: 224mph

 Price: £350,000

 Mad rating:

SSC Ultimate
Aero II

16

In 2007, American manufacturer Shelby SuperCars (SSC) took the production car speed record from the Bugatti Veyron, when its Ultimate Aero TT clocked 257mph on a closed road.

Bugatti weren't very impressed about this, and in 2009 – with the help of speed demon James May – took their Veyron Super Sports to a mighty 267mph. But SSC isn't finished yet. In 2010, it revealed the successor to the Ultimate Aero TT, a slippery, low supercar that wants to steal the production speed record back from Bugatti. With 1200bhp – that's even more than the Veyron SS – it might just do it. All it needs now is a long enough road. And a name...

 Power: *1200bhp*

 0-60mph: *Fewer than 3 seconds*

 Top speed: *More than 270mph*

 Price: *£700,000*

Mad rating: ●●●●

17 Babs

How big does an engine have to be to qualify as 'really big'? How about the 6.5-litre V12 in the Lamborghini Murcielago? Or the 8.0-litre W16 in the Bugatti Veyron? They're both midgets in comparison to the engine in Babs.

This fearsome creation featured an aeroplane engine that displaced a mighty... twenty-seven litres! Yes, twenty-seven litres. That's nearly four times the size of the Bugatti's engine. Back in 1926, British racing driver J G Parry-Thomas broke the land speed record in Babs, hitting 171mph on Pendine Sands in Wales. It was an astonishing speed in an era where crash helmets and protective clothing simply didn't exist. The next year, trying to go even quicker on the same beach, Parry-Thomas crashed at 170mph. Neither the driver nor the car survived.

 Power: 377bhp

 0-60mph: N/A

 Top speed: 171mph

 Price: £125 (in 1926)

 Mad rating:

Brabham
BT46B

How do you keep an F1 car stuck down to the track? The usual way is to use a big rear wing, which uses air pressure to 'push' the car down when it is travelling at speed.

But in the late 1970s, the Brabham engineers came up with a much sneakier idea. On the underside of their F1 car, they fitted a giant fan, which worked like a vacuum cleaner to 'suck' the bottom of the car to the track. Sounds crazy? It was, but it worked. In its first race, the 1978 Swedish Grand Prix, the BT46B took victory in the hands of Austrian racing driver Niki Lauda. However, the rest of the F1 teams complained, so the BT46B never raced again.

 Power: 520bhp

 0-60mph: 2 seconds

 Top speed: 180mph

 Price: N/A

 Mad rating:

Remember the Koenigsegg CCX, the car that spun the Stig off the track on a hot lap before it was fitted with the *Top Gear* rear wing?

Even Stig, a creature who doesn't know the meaning of the word 'fear', didn't think that car needed any more power. But that didn't stop Koenigsegg creating an even more potent hypercar. The latest weapon from the Swedish speed-merchants is built around a twin-turbo V8 with 905bhp – that's a full 100bhp more than the CCX! Koenigsegg believes the Agera could get very close to beating the Bugatti Veyron Super Sport's 267mph speed record. If it ever makes it to the *Top Gear* test track, it should push the Veyron very close for the lap record, too. Here's hoping Stig can handle it!

 Power: 905bhp

 0-60mph: 2.9 seconds

 Top speed: About 270mph

 Price: More than £500,000

 Mad rating:

19 Koenigsegg
Agera

It might have a daft name and look like it's been trapped at the bottom of a rugby scrum for a couple of years, but it's a very, very bad idea to laugh at the Gumpert Apollo.

This is a car you don't want to get on the wrong side of. Under those ugly, lumpy looks, the Apollo carries a 4.2-litre V8 borrowed from Audi... but fitted with a giant pair of turbochargers to boost power to a lethal 800bhp! Though it's legal to drive on public roads, the Gumpert feels more at home on a big, empty track, where you can fiddle around with its adjustable traction control and suspension and other complicated dials without the risk of destroying a small county.

 Power: 800bhp

 0-60mph: 3.0 seconds

 Top speed: 800mph

 Price: £250,000

 Mad rating:

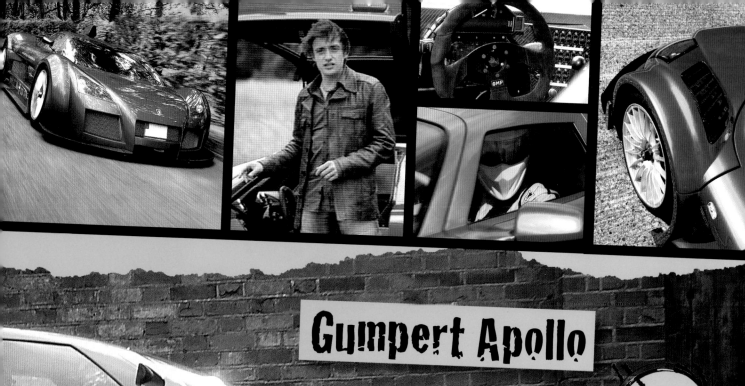

Gumpert Apollo

ortwagen-manufaktur.de

20

Versand.de

LIQUI
MOLY
MOTORENÖLE
ADDITIVE
AUTOPFLEGE

OMP

ATS
LEICHTMETALLRÄDER

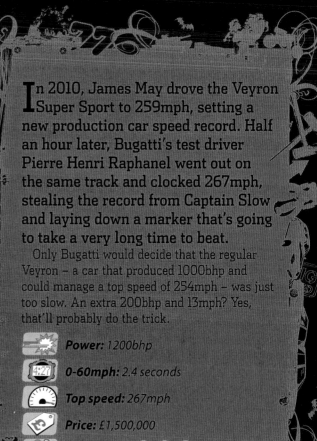

In 2010, James May drove the Veyron Super Sport to 259mph, setting a new production car speed record. Half an hour later, Bugatti's test driver Pierre Henri Raphanel went out on the same track and clocked 267mph, stealing the record from Captain Slow and laying down a marker that's going to take a very long time to beat.

Only Bugatti would decide that the regular Veyron – a car that produced 1000bhp and could manage a top speed of 254mph – was just too slow. An extra 200bhp and 13mph? Yes, that'll probably do the trick.

Power: 1200bhp

0-60mph: 2.4 seconds

Top speed: 267mph

Price: £1,500,000

Mad rating:

Bugatti Veyron
Super Sport

Porsche
918 Spyder

22

Hybrids are boring. Everyone knows that. Hybrid vehicles like the Toyota Prius and Honda Insight – which use an electric motor alongside a petrol engine for better fuel consumption and lower emissions – are very worthy and eco-friendly, but they're not exciting.

Clearly no one told Porsche. In 2010, the 918 Spyder concept shook the hybrid world like a giant earthquake. Based on a Le Mans race car, the 918 combines a 500bhp V8 with three electric motors that deliver 218bhp. That means 0-60mph in about three seconds and a top speed of 200mph. Still think hybrids are boring?

Power: 718bhp

0-60mph: 3.2 seconds

Top speed: 200mph

Price: Around £500,000

Mad rating:

When Jeremy Clarkson drove the original Ariel Atom back in 2004, it nearly ripped his face off. Obviously Ariel decided that 'nearly' wasn't really good enough, and returned in 2010 with the Atom V8 to remove Jeremy's head once and for all.

The original Atom had a 300bhp Honda engine. The Atom V8 has 500bhp. OK, that's only half the power of a Veyron, but the Atom tips the scales at just a quarter the weight of the Bugatti. It'll hit 60mph in a bit more than two seconds and revs to a motobike-like 10,000rpm. And it still doesn't have a windscreen. Be afraid.

 Power: 500bhp

 0-60mph: 2.5 seconds

 Top speed: 168mph

 Price: £140,000

 Mad rating:

Ariel Atom V8

23

Many boring small cars are front-wheel drive. But fast cars are always rear-wheel drive or four-wheel drive.

The problem with putting lots of power through the front wheels is that it becomes impossible to steer and you end up in a hedge, upside down. This didn't seem to worry the engineers at Ford when they cooked up the most powerful front-wheel drive car in the world. Based on the humble Focus but beefed up on protein shakes and raw meat, the RS500 wallops out 350bhp through its front wheels. If you can keep all that power on the road, no other Focus driver will see which way you went – especially since every RS500 is painted in the same stealthy shade of matte black!

 Power: *350bhp*

 0-60mph: *5.4 seconds*

 Top speed: *165mph*

 Price: *£36,000*

 Mad rating: 🏎🏎🏎🏎🏎

24

Ford Focus
RS500

In 2010, after eleven years of production, Pagani decided to stop building the Zonda and focus instead on producing an all-new supercar. But not before a final ultra-mad, ultra-expensive, ultra-fast send-off for one of *Top Gear*'s favourite cars.

The Cinque mixes together the best bits of the Zonda F (Pagani's fastest road car) and the Zonda R (the fastest race version) into a delicious, deranged supercar soup. It's legal to drive on the road, but with 678bhp and a top speed of 249mph – not to mention a price tag on the scary side of a million pounds – you'd better check the local speed limits very carefully!

Power: 678bhp

0-60mph: 3.4 seconds

Top speed: 249mph

Price: £1,100,000

Mad rating:

Pagani Zonda Cinque

Maserati
Boomerang

26

The Maserati Boomerang has more sharp edges than a box of kitchen knives. There isn't a curve anywhere to be found on it – well, apart from the wheels, and you get the feeling that Maserati would have made those square, too, if they could have!

The Boomerang concept looks futuristic today, so just imagine the reaction it got when it was first introduced in 1971. It didn't just look fast – it went at a mighty speed, too. With a big V8 borrowed from a Maserati race car, it could accelerate past 200mph. Then again, it looks like it's doing that speed when standing still...

Power: 310bhp

0-60mph: *Fewer than five seconds*

Top speed: *More than 200mph*

Price: £1,000,000

Mad rating: 👽👽👽👽

GTbyCitroën

27

Cars from the real world often end up in computer games. But the GTbyCitroën marks the first time that a car which started out in a computer game has made it into the real world!

When the Japanese technology wizards at Polyphony were creating the game *Gran Turismo 5* for the Playstation, they drew up a Citroën supercar with wild gull wing doors and a 780bhp fuel cell. Originally, the GTbyCitroën was only intended to exist in the virtual world, but Citroën liked it so much that they decided to build it! Unfortunately, just one GTbyCitroën was ever made, which means the closest most of us will get to driving it is on the computer...

 Power: *780bhp*

 0-60mph: *3 seconds*

 Top speed: *205mph*

 Price: *£1,500,000*

 Mad rating:

Over the years, many drivers have wished they could shut out the sound of their front-seat passenger moaning at them. In 1987, Italian engineering company Italdesign turned this wish into reality with the Aztec.

The two-seater supercar houses the driver and passenger in separate 'pods', meaning they can listen to different radio stations, though Italdesign thoughtfully included an intercom system to allow driver and passenger to communicate. The Aztec was only intended as a one-off concept car, but one Japanese company liked the design so much that it ordered 250 to be made!

 Power: *377bhp*

 0-60mph: *5.2 seconds*

 Top speed: *175mph*

 Price: *£48,000*

Mad rating:

Italdesign Aztec

Bugatti
Type 57SC Atlantic

29

It isn't very fast, it isn't very powerful and it looks a bit odd. So why is the Bugatti Type 57SC one of the maddest cars ever to have been built? Because it's the most expensive car in history.

In 2010, an anonymous bidder paid £27 million for a pristine Type 57SC. Styled by Jean Bugatti, son of the man who founded the company, it was one of just three ever built, but still... twenty-seven million pounds? For a car with less power than a modern hot hatch and no air conditioning, electric windows or heated seats? That's a mad amount of money...

 Power: 210bhp

 0-60mph: 10 seconds

 Top speed: 123mph

 Price: £27,000,000

 Mad rating:

Bentley makes some very, very fast cars, but they could never be described as mad, exactly. Apart from this one.

Back in 1999, Bentley unveiled the Hunaudières concept, a two-door supercar based on a Lamborghini Diablo. It looked slipperier and scarier than an angry python, and would have been one of the fastest cars in history. Sadly, Bentley never built it. If you think it bears a family resemblance to a slightly more famous car, you'd be right: some elements of the Hunaudières – including its 8-litre 16-cylinder engine – made their way into the Bugatti Veyron. Why? Because Volkswagen owns both Bentley and Bugatti...

30

Bentley
Hunaudières

 Power: *620bhp*

 0-60mph: *4 seconds*

 Top speed: *217mph*

 Price: Over *£250,000*

 Mad rating:

Bugatti

Galibier

31

Imagine all the fights that could have been avoided if the Galibier had been around when Jeremy raced James and Richard across France in a Veyron.

All three of them could have fitted comfortably in the same car, meaning Captain Slow and Hammond wouldn't have had to risk life and limb flying a shaky old plane over the Alps. There would even have been a spare seat for luggage. Or maps. Or *Top Gear* Dog. The Galibier is Bugatti's take on a family car: a million-pound, 217mph four-door saloon with more leather than a posh sofa shop. At the moment, it's just a concept, but Bugatti might put the Galibier into production if enough family-minded billionaires are keen. Form a queue...

 Power: *800bhp*

 0-60mph: *3 seconds*

 Top speed: *217mph*

 Price: *More than £1,000,000*

 Mad rating:

Peugeot BB1

concept

32

Modern cars are carefully constructed to protect their passengers in the unlucky event of a crash. But the Peugeot BB1 is the only car ever designed to look as if it's already been involved in a big head-on collision.

The tiny, squashy monstrosity is one of the weirdest-looking cars ever created... and one of the slowest, too. With a pair of electric motors generating just 20bhp, it won't even make it to 60mph. Peugeot says there's room in the BB1 for four adults to squeeze in, but we're not sure they'd ever make it back out...

Power: 20bhp

0-60mph: Never

Top speed: 55mph

Price: About £10,000

Mad rating: 👽👽

Very few supercars can manage more than twenty miles per gallon. Most family cars will struggle to do more than 40mpg. The Smart ForTwo diesel, the most efficient car being made at the moment, is capable of 83mpg. But the Volkswagen L1 concept can do a staggering 189mpg.

That means that this hybrid – which uses a tiny diesel engine alongside an electric motor – can travel more than 400 miles on just ten litres of diesel! OK, so it's not very fast, but at least there's seating for two... and just think: if everyone drove one of these to work, imagine how much more fuel there would be left over for the supercars...

  Power: *29bhp*

 0-60mph: *14 seconds*

 Top speed: *99mph*

 Price: *N/A*

Mad rating: 👀 👀

Volkswagen L1

33

The Corvette ZR1 is one of the maddest cars America has ever produced. But clearly even a 205mph supercar is too boring for Italian design house Bertone.

The Mantide (pronounced man-tee-day) is based on the ZR1, and uses the same 638bhp supercharged V8 engine. However, it's about 100kg lighter, while all that wild bodywork – which Bertone says was inspired by Formula One cars and jet planes – means the Mantide slices through the air far more cleanly than the Corvette. It'll manage a top speed of 217mph – that's 12mph more than the ZR1. But the Mantide's maddest figure is its price tag. At two million US dollars, it's about twenty times more expensive than the Corvette on which it is based. Ouch.

 Power: 638bhp

 0-60mph: 3.2 seconds

 Top speed: 217mph

 Price: US$2,000,000

 Mad rating:

Bertone Mantide

When it blasted onto the scene in 2007, the Furai made everything else in the history of cars look boring. Lamborghinis, Ferraris, Koenigseggs – they all appeared deathly dull beside this insane Mazda racing concept.

Based on the chassis of a Le Mans race car but armed with a super-high-revving rotary engine, the Furai made a noise like a galaxy splitting in half as it sprinted towards its top speed of 180mph. Mazda built just one single Furai, a car that mysteriously disappeared off the face of the planet just a few months later. Perhaps it was just too extreme for this world...

 Power: 450bhp

 0-60mph: 3.2 seconds

 Top speed: 180mph

 Price: £350,000

 Mad rating: 😀😀😀😀😀

Nissan Pivo

36

Reversing a car into a tight spot can be tricky. Manufacturers have come up with many clever bits of technology to help prevent drivers bashing their bumpers when parking – sensors, reversing cameras, lots of mirrors – but Nissan has come up with the maddest solution of the lot.

The cabin of the Pivo concept simply spins round on top of its wheels, meaning drivers never have to lean over their shoulders to squeeze into a narrow parking space. The name 'Pivo' is said to come from the Czech word for 'beer', which might well explain how the Nissan designers came up with this wacky concept!

Power: *75bhp*

0-60mph: *A long, long time*

Top speed: *60mph*

Price: *N/A*

Mad rating:

Toyota Aygo
Crazy

Once upon a time, Toyota used to build interesting, fast cars. But in the last few years, the world's biggest manufacturer has stuck to dull, sensible family transport. With the exception of the Aygo Crazy.

For this one-off tiny terror, the Toyota engineers ripped the tiny engine out the front of the Aygo and wedged a far bigger one, fitted with a big turbocharger, behind the front seats. Add in a load of racing bits – a roll cage, race harnesses on the seats, big arches – and that's a recipe for pint-sized thrills. And, with a £100,000 price tag, a very expensive little accident!

Power: *197bhp*

0-60mph: *5.9 seconds*

Top speed: *127mph*

Price: *£100,000*

Mad rating: 😎😎😎

KTM X-Bow R

38

KTM is famous around the world for building motorbikes. The X-Bow is the first car ever produced by the Austrian firm, but it's the nearest thing to a superbike with four wheels.

With a pumped-up version of the turbocharged engine from an Audi S3 sat right behind the driver's head and a lightweight body made of carbon fibre and plastic, the X-Bow is light, fast and seriously intense. With no windscreen to protect you, every fly, wasp and mosquito on the road becomes a speeding bullet. Wear a helmet or prepare to be splattered by insects!

 Power: 300bhp

 0-60mph: 3.9 seconds

 Top speed: 135mph

 Price: More than £50,000

 Mad rating:

Stuff is bigger in the USA. Burgers. Buildings. And, of course, the cars. The Hummer H1 – an off-roader originally built for the American army but converted for use by civilians – is one of the very biggest.

Nearly five-metres long and two-metres high, it weighs in at more than three tonnes and struggles to do more than five miles on a gallon of petrol. On the plus side, Hummers are almost indestructible, and can wade through almost three feet of water and scramble up near-vertical slopes. Good luck finding a big enough parking space in the local supermarket, though!

 Power: *300bhp*

 0-60mph: *13.5 seconds*

 Top speed: *90mph*

 Price: *£100,000*

 Mad rating:

39

Hummer H1

In 2009, Peugeot won the 24 Hours of Le Mans with a race car powered by a huge diesel engine.

But this giant engine – with nearly four times as much torque as a Lamborghini Gallardo – wasn't only to be found in an endurance race car. Oh no. In a completely sensible and in no way mad move, Peugeot also jammed the V12 turbodiesel into a four seat luxury car that could sprint from 0-60mph in just three seconds. That's an insane figure for a big diesel car. Unfortunately, the 908 RC never made it to production, perhaps because Peugeot feared it would simply turn its tyres into smoke!

 Power: 690bhp

 0-60mph: 3 seconds

 Top speed: 186mph

 Price: N/A

 Mad rating:

Peugeot
908 RC
40

Prodrive p2

Jeremy Clarkson is made of strong stuff. He's thrashed nearly every modern supercar around the *Top Gear* test track, speeding, sliding and spinning them until their tyres give up. Not one of them has made him feel even a little bit queasy. Apart from this one.

When he tested it back in 2006, the Prodrive P2 made Jeremy vomit from motion sickness. The two-seater P2, which uses the turbo-mad engine from a Subaru Impreza STi, has a clever four-wheel drive system that allows it to corner faster and tighter than just about any other car in history. Great news for a quick lap time, not such good news for Jeremy's stomach!

Power: *344bhp*

0-60mph: *3.8 seconds*

Top speed: *174mph*

Price: *About £50,000*

Mad rating:

Bristol
Fighter T

42

It might look like it was built in a shed in the 1970s, but don't be fooled: the Bristol Fighter T is a true hypercar.

With a V10 engine borrowed from the Dodge Viper, but with a huge turbocharger bolted on, it produces 1,017bhp – that's more than the Bugatti Veyron! Bristol says the Fighter T is capable of 270mph, but is limited to 225mph for safety reasons. You would think that, with numbers like that, the Fighter T might be more famous, but Bristol is a mysterious company. The British company is more secretive than MI6, refusing to reveal even how many cars they sell! If you ever spot a Fighter T on the road, think yourself very lucky – and best of luck keeping up with it!

 Power: *1,017bhp*

 0-60mph: *3 seconds*

 Top speed: *225mph*

 Price: *£350,000*

Mad rating: 🦷🦷🦷🦷

In 2001, Aston Martin asked the famous designer Giorgetto Giugiaro – the man responsible for some of Ferrari, Maserati and Alfa Romeo's most beautiful cars – what he thought an Aston convertible would look like in the year 2020.

Giugiaro came back with this, the Aston Martin 2020 concept. It might look like a two-seater, but the cover underneath the 2020's shiny roll hoop can be removed to reveal a couple of small seats. It was fast, too – Giugiaro didn't think cars in the future would be powered by hydrogen or electricity, but instead a huge V12 engine with a supercharger. Was he right? We'll have to hang on a few more years to find out...

Power: *470bhp*

0-60mph: *Fewer than 4 seconds*

Top speed: *180mph*

Price: *N/A*

Mad rating:

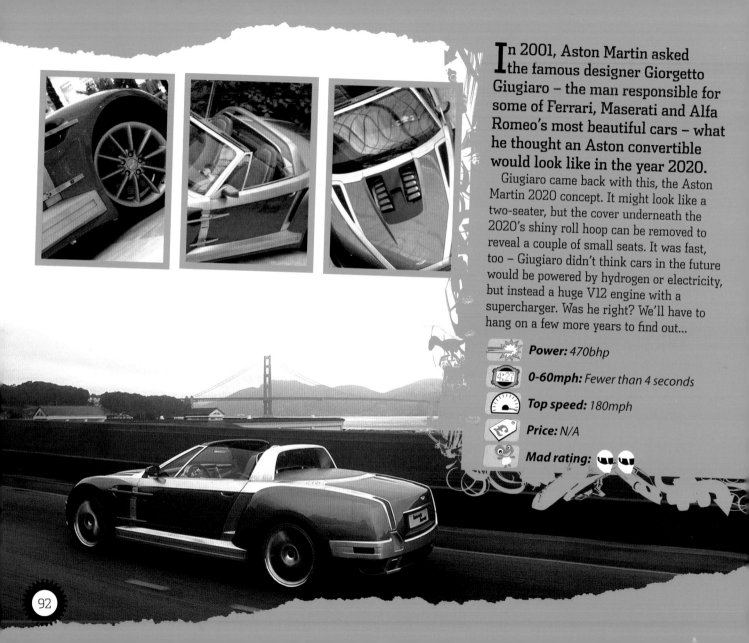

Aston Martin
2020

43

Is this the weirdest-looking car in the history of the world? It might well be. When James May drove the Mitsuoka Orochi in Japan in 2008, he praised it for being quiet and comfortable. However, he didn't mention anything about the appearance of this sort-of-supercar, which was probably for the best.

The Orochi looks like a cross between an evil dragon and some sort of sad deep water fish. A horrible mix of curves and wings with a funny little mouth on the front, it's the sort of car that makes pedestrians run screaming in the opposite direction, clutching their eyes and feeling sick. And, with a not-very-powerful 3.3-litre V6 under the bonnet, the Orochi isn't even quick enough to outrun all the insults!

 Power: 280bhp

 0-60mph: 6 seconds

 Top speed: 170mph

 Price: £44,000

 Mad rating:

Mitsuoka Orochi

'Every time you stamp on the throttle, this thing just drop kicks your stomach half a mile back down the road!' yelled Richard Hammond when he tested the Veritas RS3 in 2008.

That blistering acceleration is thanks to a 473bhp BMW V8 under that long, long bonnet, but it's the way the Veritas looks that really wallops you in the stomach. Richard described it as 'a 1930s racing car from the future', which isn't as crazy as it sounds: Veritas built Germany's first Formula One car back in 1951. If you see the glinting, grinning face of the RS3 looming in your rear mirror, best move out of the way quickly!

Power: *473bhp*

0-60mph: *3.6 seconds*

Top speed: *216mph*

Price: *£247,000*

Mad rating:

Veritas
RS3

45

For two decades, the Dodge Viper has been one of America's scariest, lairiest supercars, with a reputation for being more dangerous than a hungry lion with toothache. But the ACR version makes the standard Viper look like a fluffy kitten.

This is a race car for the road, with more power, less weight and a rear wing bigger than a park bench. Inside the ACR, there's... well, there's not very much at all. No stereo, no carpets, no speakers – just a digital timer for recording exactly how fast you've just gone round the *Top Gear* test track. Scared? You should be...

 Power: *600bhp*

 0-60mph: *3.2 seconds*

 Top speed: *203mph*

 Price: *£54,000*

 Mad rating:

46

Dodge Viper

ACR

Stirling Moss was one of Britain's greatest-ever racing drivers, winning sixteen Grands Prix in the 1950s and 60s at a time when Formula One racing was more deadly than wrestling with a great white shark.

So, when McLaren and Mercedes decided to honour Sir Stirling in 2008 with a new car, obviously they needed to cook up something a bit more extreme than a diesel supermini! They came up with this, the SLR Stirling Moss 722. It looks like a huge, silvery bullet and travels very nearly as fast, with a top speed of 217mph. With no windscreen, that's an experience sure to make your eyes water, as is the price – the SLR Stirling Moss costs more than £800,000!

 Power: *641bhp*

 0-60mph: *3.5 seconds*

 Top speed: *217mph*

Price: *£815,000*

Mad rating:

47

Mercedes-McLaren SLR
Stirling Moss 722

48

Porsche engineers are often accused of being too serious and not having a sense of humour. But take a look at the paintjob on this 917 race car from 1971. Nicknamed the 'Pink Pig', it was painted with the names of the cuts of meat from a pig, like a butcher's diagram!

Even without the bizarre paintjob, the Porsche 917 was a monstrous car. One of the most successful endurance racers ever, it won the 24 Hours of Le Mans in 1970 and 1971, recording over 240mph in the process. By the end of its life, the 917 could produce over 1,500bhp – and was described by drivers as a 'pig' to drive. Maybe that's not so surprising...

Power: 1,500bhp

0-60mph: Fewer than 3 seconds

Top speed: 240mph

Price: N/A

Mad rating:

Renault 5 Maxi Turbo
Group B rally car

49

The early 1980s was a mad time for rallying. In 1982, the organisers of world rallying drew up a new set of rules and regulations that read something like this: 'Do whatever you want'.

The new category was called 'Group B', and saw some of the most powerful, scariest rally cars ever produced. The Renault 5 Maxi Turbo was one of the maddest of the bunch. It was based on Renault's tiny city car of the day, and though it only had a little 1.4-litre turbo engine mounted behind the driver, it produced a beefy 350bhp. The Maxi slipped and slid its way to victory over bigger, more powerful cars on dirt, tarmac and snow all around the world.

Power: *350bhp*

0-60mph: *3 seconds*

Top speed: *About 130mph*

Price: *N/A*

Mad rating:

Auto Union
Type C

In the 1930s, manufacturers Mercedes and Auto Union (the German company that eventually became Audi in the 1960s) engaged in a battle to build the fastest car in the world. Their rivals were scary, sleek supercars with huge amounts of power by the standards of the day, and the Auto Union Type C was the scariest of the bunch.

In 1938, young driver Bernd Rosemeyer clocked an amazing 270mph in the 500bhp Type C on a closed section of the German autobahn, just beating the Mercedes record of 268mph that had been set earlier the same day. Tragically, though it was powerful enough, Rosemeyer's car couldn't handle the speed and span off the road, killing him. No one ever attempted a record attempt in the Type C again.

 Power: 550bhp

 0-60mph: N/A

 Top speed: 270mph

 Price: N/A

 Mad rating: 👹👹👹👹

Blower Bentley

51

GT 8771

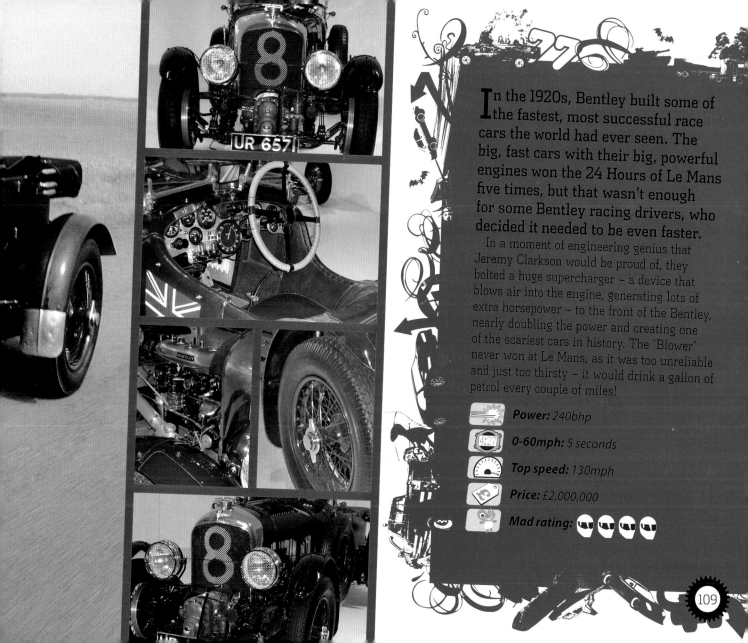

In the 1920s, Bentley built some of the fastest, most successful race cars the world had ever seen. The big, fast cars with their big, powerful engines won the 24 Hours of Le Mans five times, but that wasn't enough for some Bentley racing drivers, who decided it needed to be even faster.

In a moment of engineering genius that Jeremy Clarkson would be proud of, they bolted a huge supercharger – a device that blows air into the engine, generating lots of extra horsepower – to the front of the Bentley, nearly doubling the power and creating one of the scariest cars in history. The 'Blower' never won at Le Mans, as it was too unreliable and just too thirsty – it would drink a gallon of petrol every couple of miles!

Power: 240bhp

0-60mph: 5 seconds

Top speed: 130mph

Price: £2,000,000

Mad rating:

52

Benetton B186
F1 car

Big engines are more powerful than small engines. The two-litre engine in a VW Golf GTI produces about 200bhp, while the six-litre engine in the Ferrari 599 produces about 600bhp. So take a guess how much power was produced by the tiny 1.5-litre engine in Benetton's 1986 F1 car. Ready for this? 1500bhp.

That's one-and-a-half times as much as the Bugatti Veyron, in an engine one-fifth the size. How did they manage it? With a huge turbocharger and some very brave drivers. 'You felt like you were sitting on a rocket,' said Benetton driver Gerhard Berger. The B186 was one of the fastest F1 cars of its day, but only recorded a single victory because it kept blowing up!

 Power: *1500bhp*

 0-60mph: *2 seconds*

 Top speed: *217mph*

 Price: *N/A*

 Mad rating:

53

TVR Cerbera
Speed 12

TVR has long had a reputation for producing some of Britain's most fearsome sports cars, vehicles driven with teeth gritted and hands clenched around the wheel in fear.

But TVR never built a car more teeth-gritting or hand-clenching than this one. First shown to the world in 1997, the Cerbera Speed 12 was built around a giant 7.7-litre V12 engine that churned out nearly 1000bhp – the biggest, most powerful engine TVR had ever built. The Speed 12 was believed to have a top speed of about 240mph, but no one was ever brave enough to find out – the car was just too extreme to drive on the road, so just one was ever built!

 Power: 950bhp

 0-60mph: 2.9 seconds

 Top speed: 240mph

 Price: £188,000

 Mad rating:

Rover Metro 6R4
rally car

The Rover Metro was one of the most boring cars of the 1980s. But the rally version – which competed against the Renault 5 Maxi Turbo – was one of the very maddest.

Somehow, Rover managed to pack nearly 400bhp and four-wheel drive into the Metro's tiny body, creating a rally car that weighed nearly nothing but accelerated like a space rocket. OK, so the Metro never actually won a world rally event, and it was mainly made of flimsy plastic, but who cares about that when it has a front wing that looks like a snowplough?

 Power: *390bhp*

 0-60mph: *Fewer than three seconds*

 Top speed: *About 130mph*

 Price: *N/A*

 Mad rating: 🂠🂠🂠🂠

Lamborghini Diablo

55

Jeremy Clarkson described the Diablo as 'the biggest head-turner in the world'. If you want to sneak around unnoticed, this car shouldn't be at the top of your shopping list – it's about as subtle as a rhinoceros wearing a police siren on its head!

And it has the go to match the show – when it was introduced in 1990, the Diablo (which means 'Devil' in Italian) was the fastest car in the world, beating the Ferrari F40's previous record of 201mph with its top speed of 207mph. And the F40 didn't have a very cool set of scissor doors, either...

 Power: *492bhp*

 0-60mph: *3.9 seconds*

 Top speed: *207mph*

 Price: *£130,000*

 Mad rating:

A Lamborghini off-roader? Really? You'd better believe your eyes. In 1986, the Lambo engineers got bored of building supercars and rolled out this giant 4x4 instead.

The LM002 was based on a near-indestructible military vehicle and weighed nearly three tonnes, so despite its big V12 engine it was a slow old beast... especially by Lamborghini's standards! However, for the millionaire customers that needed more speed from their giant, expensive Lamborghini off-roader, the LM002 could be ordered with a 500bhp engine... from a racing powerboat! After building just 300 LM002s, Lamborghini decided it was better at making supercars after all...

Power: 450bhp

0-60mph: 7.8 seconds

Top speed: 126mph

Price: £80,000

Mad rating:

Lamborghini
LM002

56

57

Ferrari
FXX

This is the car that Michael 'The Stig' Schumacher took round the *Top Gear* test track in the astonishing time of 1m 10.7s. The FXX's time wasn't allowed to stand on the Power Laps board – it has slick racing tyres, which aren't allowed on the road – but it might still be the maddest car Ferrari has ever made.

The FXX is based on the road-legal Enzo, but it is even more extreme: its V12 engine cranks out more than 800bhp and propels the FXX to a top speed of nearly 250mph! Ferrari originally promised to build twenty-nine FXXs, but eventually built just one more, which was presented to Michael Schumacher when he left the Ferrari F1 team in 2006. Not a bad leaving present...

Power: *850bhp*

0-60mph: *2.8 seconds*

Top speed: *249mph*

Price: *£1,500,000*

Mad rating:

John Hennessey is an American tuner. He takes fast cars and makes them even faster.

Usually he modifies American vehicles, but for his maddest creation ever, he chose one of Britain's finest sports cars, the Lotus Exige. The standard Exige, though it only produces about 200bhp, is still supercar-fast because it's so light. However, Hennessey decided it needed more power. A lot more power. Somehow, he managed to fit the V8 engine from a Corvette into the middle of the Exige, an engine that makes... 1000bhp. Five times the power of the Exige. Hennessey reckons the Venom could, in theory, do a ridiculous 272mph, but there aren't many drivers in the world brave enough to find out...

 Power: 1000bhp

 0-60mph: 2.4 seconds

 Top speed: 272mph

 Price: Around £600,000

 Mad rating:

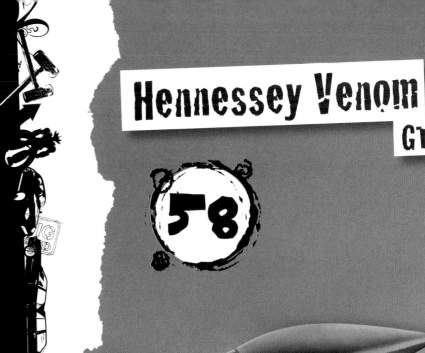

Hennessey Venom GT

58

123

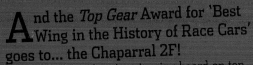

And the *Top Gear* Award for 'Best Wing in the History of Race Cars' goes to... the Chaparral 2F!

Even without the giant ironing board on top, the 2F was a mad thing. It was the first racer to be made of lightweight fibreglass, and packed a giant V8 for good measure. But when Chaparral bolted that huge wing to the back of the 2F, it went from being a merely mad race car to one of the daftest things ever seen on a track. The driver could control the angle of the wing on the move, using a pedal by his left foot. The 2F was fast, too, winning dozens of races in the late 1960s.

 Power: 525bhp

 0-60mph: 3.6 seconds

 Top speed: 198mph

 Price: N/A

 Mad rating:

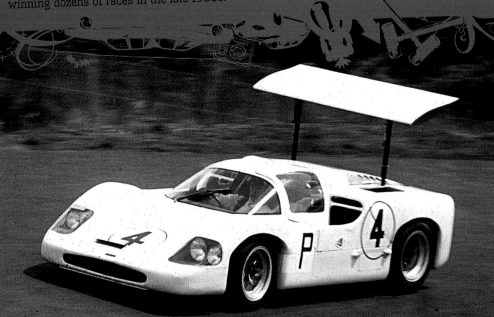

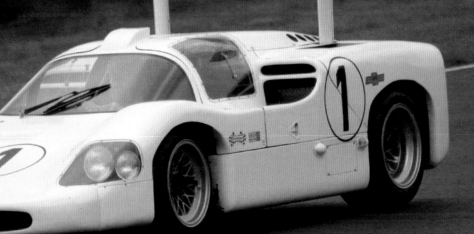

Chaparral
2F

Transit SuperVan

60

What do the engineers at Ford do when they've finished their day jobs building the Focus RS and GT40s? They relax with a nice cup of tea... and set about turning Transit vans into supercars.

Since 1971, Ford has built three generations of SuperVan, and they've all been as bonkers as... well, as bonkers as a big builder's van with a race car engine jammed in the middle! The first SuperVan borrowed the 400bhp engine from Ford's Le Mans race car, while the second and third SuperVans used 650bhp Formula One engines and could do 180mph flat-out. Sadly, none of the SuperVans was road-legal, but just think how many plumbers would have got to work early if they had been!

 Power: 650bhp

 0-60mph: Fewer than 3 seconds

 Top speed: 174mph

 Price: N/A

 Mad rating:

61

Mercedes
300SL

128

Even alongside bonkers twenty-first century supercars like the Lamborghini Murcielago and Pagani Zonda, the Mercedes 300SL looks wild. Imagine how radical it must have seemed when it was introduced in 1955, on the road next to VW Beetles and Morris Minors.

With its beautiful 'gull wings' – so-called because, with its doors open, the Mercedes looked like a seagull in flight – the 300SL was one of the first true supercars and the fastest car in the world when it was introduced. The 300SL was the inspiration for Mercedes' new SLS supercar, but the original will cost you far, far more – a perfect example could set you back a cool million pounds!

 Power: 240bhp

 0-60mph: 7.2 seconds

 Top speed: 165mph

 Price: £100,000 to £1,000,000

 Mad rating:

If you're thinking that the Dauer 962 looks like a Le Mans race car, you'd be exactly right. It is. In fact, a very similar 962 won the 24-hour race in 1994.

But there's something special about the 962 on the page in front of you. It's road-legal. This monster is permitted to drive on public roads. And park at the supermarket. And do all those things that normal, sensible hatchbacks are allowed to do. With its 730bhp race engine, the Dauer can accelerate to 120mph in fewer than eight seconds and won't run out of steam until it hits 250mph. You're allowed to drive it on the road, but whether you'd want to is a different matter!

 Power: 730bhp

 0-60mph: 2.6 seconds

 Top speed: 250mph

 Price: £700,000

  **Mad rating:**

Dauer 962
Le Mans

62

N·CM 962

The Aston Martin One-77 costs £1,200,000. That is a crazy amount of money, but the One-77 is a crazy machine.

At 750bhp, it is the most powerful naturally aspirated road car in the world in other words, with the most powerful engine not to use a turbocharger or a supercharger. It is made from carbon fibre and has lots of gold leaf in its engine. It will hit 60mph in a bit over three seconds and keep accelerating way past 200mph. And it will be a rarer sight than seeing Jeremy Clarkson lost for words: just seventy-seven cars will ever be built. Worth £1.2 million? Those seventy-seven lucky owners will definitely think so...

 Power: *750bhp*

 0-60mph: *Fewer than 3.5 seconds*

 Top speed: *More than 200mph*

 Price: *£1,200,000*

 Mad rating: 👽👽👽

Aston Martin
One-77

63

Wood is a good material for making many things. Tables. Cupboards. Saunas. But not cars. American designer Joe Harmon wants to change that.

He's built this 240mph supercar almost entirely from bits of tree, just to show what can be done with wood. The Splinter's wheels, suspension and body panels are all made from the stuff. Harmon says that, when used in the right place, wood is stronger than steel or aluminium – and, of course, it can be recycled too! It might be a few years before we see a wooden supercar on the road, but if we do, just watch out for woodworm. And matches.

Power: 377bhp

0-60mph: 3 seconds

Top speed: 240mph

Price: N/A

Mad rating: 😀😀😀

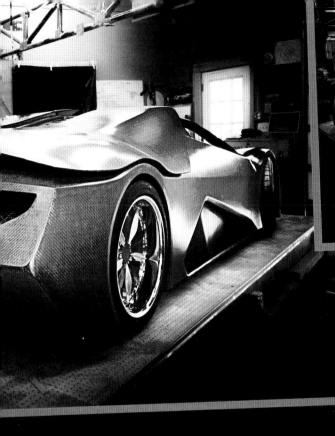

Joe Harmon

Splinter

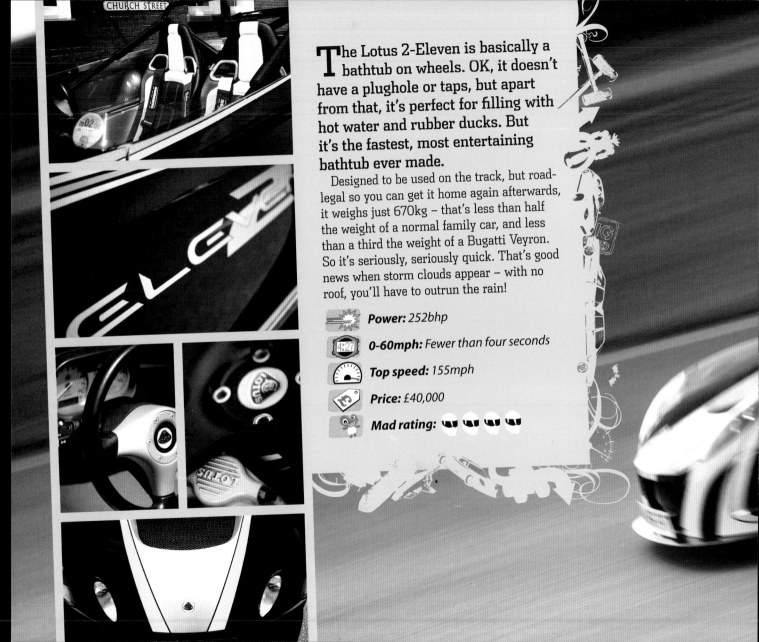

The Lotus 2-Eleven is basically a bathtub on wheels. OK, it doesn't have a plughole or taps, but apart from that, it's perfect for filling with hot water and rubber ducks. But it's the fastest, most entertaining bathtub ever made.

Designed to be used on the track, but road-legal so you can get it home again afterwards, it weighs just 670kg – that's less than half the weight of a normal family car, and less than a third the weight of a Bugatti Veyron. So it's seriously, seriously quick. That's good news when storm clouds appear – with no roof, you'll have to outrun the rain!

Power: *252bhp*

0-60mph: *Fewer than four seconds*

Top speed: *155mph*

Price: *£40,000*

Mad rating:

Lotus 2-Eleven

65

In 1994, the McLaren F1 road car clocked a top speed of 231mph, a production record that stood for eleven years until the Koenigsegg CCR managed 240mph in 2005.

That amazing record is just one of the reasons that the McLaren is recognised as one of the greatest road cars ever, but it was also one of the greatest race cars, too. In fact, because it was such a brilliant road car to start with, it didn't need many modifications to become a champion racer. In 1995, the F1 GTR won the greatest endurance race in the world, the 24 Hours of Le Mans, hitting 198mph during the race. What a car!

66

McLaren
F1 GTR

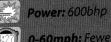
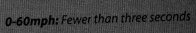
Power: *600bhp*

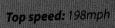
0-60mph: *Fewer than three seconds*

Top speed: *198mph*

Price: *N/A*

Mad rating: 👺👺👺

Top Fuel Dragsters are the fastest-accelerating cars in the world. From a standing start on a drag strip, they can hit 60mph in 0.7 seconds and can reach 330mph in fewer than four seconds. Imagine that.

From zero to 330mph in the time it takes to write your name. Top Fuel cars use 8.2-litre V8 engines that run on something called nitromethane – a fuel that's also an explosive! In other words, the engine of a Top Fuel Dragster is a bomb. What sort of skills do you need to strap yourself to the front of one of these bombs and fire down a drag strip? A lot of bravery, for a start. A large dose of stupidity might come in handy, too!

 Power: *10,000bhp*

 0-60mph: *0.7 seconds*

 Top speed: *330mph*

 Price: *£50,000 per engine*

 Mad rating:

67

Top Fuel Dragster

58

Reliant Robin

Most of the cars in this book are fast. Some of them are very fast. The Reliant Robin isn't. In fact, it isn't even technically a car.

British company Reliant built the Robin with just three wheels because that meant it technically qualified as a motorcycle. If only it was as fast as a motorcycle. With its tiny engine, the Reliant took nearly twenty seconds to reach 60mph and had a maximum speed of just 85mph – unless you were at the top of a very steep hill, in which case you might get nearer to 90mph. The Reliant's three-wheel design also meant that it was occasionally prone to tipping over, as Jeremy Clarkson discovered on a test drive in 2010!

 Power: *32bhp*

 0-60mph: *18.5 seconds*

 Top speed: *85mph*

 Price: *£500*

 Mad rating: 👓👓

In the last sixty years, BMW has made some of the fastest, best-handling sports cars on the planet. It also made this, the Isetta.

It may look like a toy car, but during the 1950s the Isetta was one of the best-selling microcars in Europe. It measured only 230cm from nose to tail and used a tiny single-cylinder engine that produced just 13bhp, which didn't provide very much performance with two people on-board. No one ever discovered the 0-60mph time of the Isetta – not because they were too scared to take it on the motorway, but because its top speed was 55mph!

 Power: *13bhp*

 0-60mph: *Never*

 Top speed: *55mph*

 Price: *£415*

 Mad rating:

BMW Isetta

69

As Britain discovers every winter, normal cars aren't much good in the snow, slipping and sliding around helpless as soon as the white stuff starts to fall. But the Subaru STI TRAX is a bit different.

Like a piste basher in a ski resort, it's fitted with four giant snow tracks instead of tyres. But unlike a piste basher, it also has a 400bhp Subaru turbo engine, making it as fast over snow as the normal Subaru Impreza STi is on the tarmac. Which lucky driver gets to thrash this mean machine over the mountains? That'll be Ken Block, the rally driver that scared the pants off James May back in 2009...

 Power: *400bhp*

 0-60mph: *Fewer than 6 seconds on snow!*

 Top speed: *Unspecified*

 Price: *N/A*

 Mad rating:

Subaru STi

TRAX

 70

Pontiac Aztek

Turn the page. Cover your eyes. Flush this book down the toilet. Whatever you do, don't look at the Pontiac for too long, or you'll risk permanent damage to your eyes.

This American 4x4, first released in 2001, must have the ugliest face of any car ever built. Quite how Pontiac's design team came up with this monstrous creation – and allowed it to go into production – remains a mystery. Just be glad it isn't around any more. On the plus side, the Aztek's hideous front end even manages to make the Mitsuoka Orochi look quite nice!

 Power: 185bhp

 0-60mph: 9.2 seconds

 Top speed: 108mph

 Price: £15,000

 Mad rating:

Most cars are built for about six or seven years before being replaced. Some may have a lifespan of ten years. But the Trabant – a cheap, cruddy family car from East Germany – was built continuously for thirty years!

Even when it was first released under communist rule in 1957, the Trabant wasn't considered very high-tech – its 30bhp two-cylinder engine had been originally designed before the Second World War. By the time production finally finished in the late 1980s, the Trabant looked as if it came from another century, or perhaps millennium. Still, it was popular – over three million Trabants were built, with waiting lists stretching for fifteen years in the 1960s!

 Power: 30bhp

 0-60mph: 30 seconds

 Top speed: 62mph

 Price: £350

 Mad rating:

Trabant

72

151

Bugatti spent many, many millions of pounds developing the 254mph Veyron. So they can't have been very impressed when, in 2007, the Veyron's speed record was beaten by an American newcomer built for a fraction of the cost.

The Ultimate Aero TT clocked a mighty 256mph on a closed road in Washington State, USA, to become the fastest production car in the world. If you haven't heard of SSC, you're not alone. Shelby SuperCars, to give the company its full name, is a tiny American outfit that has built just a few dozen cars since it was set up ten years ago. But that didn't stop them going out and giving the mighty Veyron a damn good thrashing. Want to know how much that angered Bugatti? Look up the Veyron Super Sports to find out!

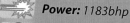 **Power:** 1183bhp

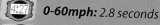 **0-60mph:** 2.8 seconds

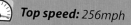 **Top speed:** 256mph

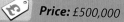 **Price:** £500,000

 **Mad rating:**

SSC Ultimate
Aero TT

73

The Beast

74

The President of the United States is the most powerful man in the world. That means he needs a lot of protection.

Barack Obama's Cadillac limousine – nicknamed 'The Beast' – is probably the safest car in the history of the world. Its armour-plated doors are eight inches thick and can withstand an attack from a rocket launcher, while the tyres are made of Kevlar. The Beast is equipped with tear gas cannons and night vision cameras, but all that armour-plating means it's seriously heavy: despite its 6.5-litre diesel engine, it'll still take fifteen seconds to reach 60mph!

 Power: 400bhp

 0-60mph: 15 seconds

 Top speed: 60mph

 Price: £300,000

 Mad rating:

Porsche makes so many different 911s that it sometimes becomes difficult to tell them apart. Here's what makes the GT2 RS different: it's the most powerful road car Porsche has ever built.

Its turbocharged engine produces a walloping 611bhp, good for a top speed of 205mph, and it has lots of lightweight carbon fibre bits to keep weight to a minimum. Most powerful turbocharged Porsches are four-wheel drive – meaning better safety and grip – but the GT2 RS is strictly rear-wheel drive. That means it's fast, slidey and decidedly dangerous. This isn't just the most powerful Porsche ever – it's the maddest, too!

 Power: *611bhp*

 0-60mph: *3.5 seconds*

 Top speed: *205mph*

 Price: *£165,000*

 Mad rating:

Porsche 911

GT2 RS

75

It looks like something that a three-year-old might pedal round the garden in, but the Brutsch Mopetta is a real, road-legal car.

It was built in Germany between 1956 and 1958, and was powered by a tiny single-cylinder engine that produced – ready for this? – less than two horsepower! The Mopetta weighed just 78kg – about the same as a grown man – and with three wheels and a top speed of 28mph, you had to be seriously brave, or seriously daft, to take it out on public roads. Not many were brave or daft enough: only fourteen Mopettas were ever made.

 Power: *1.8bhp*

 0-60mph: *Never*

 Top speed: *28mph*

 Price: *£200*

 Mad rating: 😎😎😎

Brutsch Mopetta

77

Citroën 2CV
Sahara

The Citroën 2CV was a simple, cheap, French car first made in 1948. With a small engine driving the front wheels, it was surprisingly good at trundling down tracks and over fields.

But when customers demanded a 2CV that could deal with really difficult off-road terrain, what did Citroën do? They stuck another engine in the boot, of course. The 2CV Sahara was a double-engined 4x4 that could scramble up mountains or over deserts... but had absolutely nowhere to put your shopping! You might think that, with two engines, the 2CV would be seriously powerful. It wasn't. Each of its engines produced just 14bhp, giving it a total power output of 28bhp!

 Power: *28bhp*

 0-60mph: *Never!*

 Top speed: *49mph*

 Price: *£400*

 Mad rating:

Venturi Eclectic

78

You might think you're looking at a daft concept from the 1930s, but the Venturi Eclectic is actually straight out of the twenty-first century.

Designed to be the greenest car on the planet, the Eclectic has both a solar panel and a wind turbine fitted, so when you park up, it can use the energy of both the sun and the wind to recharge its electric batteries. A great idea, with just a few problems. First, it has a top speed of just 30mph. Secondly, it looks ridiculous. And thirdly, what happens if you park your car in a dark garage?

Power: 28bhp

0-60mph: Never

Top speed: 30mph

Price: N/A

Mad rating:

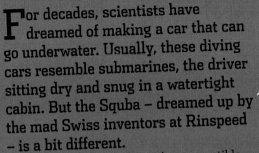

For decades, scientists have dreamed of making a car that can go underwater. Usually, these diving cars resemble submarines, the driver sitting dry and snug in a watertight cabin. But the Squba – dreamed up by the mad Swiss inventors at Rinspeed – is a bit different.

Based on the Lotus Elise, it's a convertible, meaning that the driver and passenger will get soaking wet as soon as the Squba dives below the surface of the water! There's an oxygen supply on-board, so at least they'll be able to breathe – but won't the salt water make a horrible mess of their clothes? Not to mention their sandwiches...

 Power: 73bhp

 0-60mph: 12 seconds

 Top speed: 81mph

 Price: Under £300,000

 Mad rating:

79

Rinspeed
Squba

This isn't a spaceship from a science fiction film. This is one of the weirdest supercars in the world... and one of the fastest!

Made by a small Spanish company, the Tramontana R looks like a jet fighter and packs military firepower, with a Mercedes V12 squeezed into the back and blasting out a deadly 720bhp. There's room for two on-board, though the passenger has to sit directly behind the driver. No, they won't be able to see much of what's happening on the road, but then again, with a 0-60mph time of fewer than four seconds, the view of the road ahead will probably be a bit of a blur for the driver, too!

Power: 720bhp

0-60mph: 3.6 seconds

Top speed: 186mph

Price: £33,000

Mad rating: 🏁🏁🏁🏁

Tramontana

R

80

TRAMONTAN

81

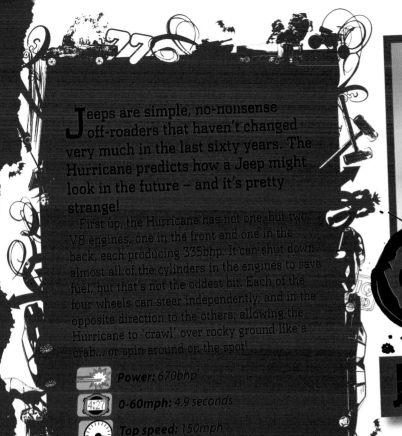

Jeeps are simple, no-nonsense off-roaders that haven't changed very much in the last sixty years. The Hurricane predicts how a Jeep might look in the future – and it's pretty strange!

First up, the Hurricane has not one, but two V8 engines, one in the front and one in the back, each producing 335bhp. It can shut down almost all of the cylinders in the engines to save fuel, but that's not the oddest bit. Each of the four wheels can steer independently, and in the opposite direction to the others, allowing the Hurricane to 'crawl' over rocky ground like a crab... or spin around on the spot!

Power: 670bhp

0-60mph: 4.9 seconds

Top speed: 150mph

Price: N/A

Mad rating: ⚫⚫⚫

Jeep Hurricane

82

Gemballa Tornado

When tuners carry out modifications to a new car, it's usually to make it faster or handle better. But when the German engineers at Gemballa got hold of a Porsche Cayenne, their only intention seems to have been to make it even uglier!

The standard Cayenne isn't a pretty car, exactly, but it looks like an Alfa Romeo 8C beside the disgusting Tornado, a car that resembles a melted mechanical hippo. At least the Gemballa has more power and pace than a normal Cayenne – useful when you're trying to escape the crowds of people throwing tomatoes and eggs at your pig-ugly car...

 Power: 750bhp

 0-60mph: 4.3 seconds

 Top speed: 186mph

 Price: £400,000

Mad rating:

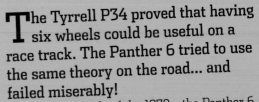

The Tyrrell P34 proved that having six wheels could be useful on a race track. The Panther 6 tried to use the same theory on the road... and failed miserably!

By the standards of the 1970s, the Panther 6 was very high-tech, with an on-board telephone and television included as standard, and absurdly quick. With an 8.2-litre V8 sitting between those front four wheels, it was claimed to be capable of 200mph, though no one was ever foolish enough to test that claim. The only problem was that no one wanted to buy it: just two Panther 6s were ever made. Oops.

 Power: *600bhp*

 0-60mph: *4.8 seconds*

 Top speed: *200mph*

 Price: *N/A*

 Mad rating:

Panther 6

83

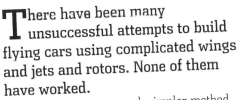

There have been many unsuccessful attempts to build flying cars using complicated wings and jets and rotors. None of them have worked.

The Skycar uses a much simpler method for getting off the ground: it's a dune buggy with a big fan bolted to the back... all attached to the wing from a paraglider. It might seem to be a daft solution, but it works: in 2009, the Parajet team flew – and drove – 3700 miles from London to Timbuktu in Africa! But even if you're not planning on crossing continents in your flying car, think what quick work it would make of motorway traffic jams...

 Power: *140bhp*

 0-60mph: *4.2 seconds*

 Top speed: *140mph*

 Price: *N/A*

 Mad rating:

 **84** Parajet Skycar

The F350 Super Duty truck is the longest and tallest car in the world. From tip to tail, it measures an obscene 665cm – considerably more than twice the length of a Mini – and stands more than two metres tall!

It weighs more than three tonnes, and that's before you load up that huge flat-bed with rocks and tools and fast food and all the other stuff that American trucks have to transport. No wonder the F350 Super Duty gets a giant V8 engine – anything smaller and it wouldn't even get moving! Don't think that this is an old-fashioned pick-up, though. It even comes with an on-board computer connected to the Internet – perfect for finding out where the nearest drive-through burger joint is!

 Power: 385bhp

 0-60mph: 8.5 seconds

 Top speed: 95mph

 Price: £45,000

 Mad rating:

Ford F350
Super Duty

85

It looks like a bin lorry crossed with a tractor , but the Unimog is one of the biggest, most indestructible vehicles on the planet.

This giant 4x4 is generally found in the most extreme environments on Earth – jungles, deserts, mountains, even Wales – and is used by fire fighters and the military to get to places that normal vehicles simply can't reach. Weighing more than four tonnes and standing 273cm tall, the Unimog is also a mean off-road racer and has competed in the Dakar rally. In other words, you don't want to get on the wrong side of one of these: they're big, they're fast and there's absolutely nowhere they can't reach!

 Power: 260bhp

 0-60mph: 20 seconds

 Top speed: 63mph

 Price: £75,000

 Mad rating:

Unimog
U5000

86

You could go to the shops in the Impreza Cosworth. Put your grocery bags in the boot. Drop Grandma off at bingo. With five doors and five seats, the Impreza Cosworth does a nice impression of a family hatchback.

But then, when you found an empty road and pressed the accelerator to the floor, you'd find out that the Impreza Cosworth is a screaming, evil supercar in the body of a nice family hatchback. With a 400bhp turbo engine lurking under that bonnet, it'll flatten the 0-60mph sprint in 3.7 seconds and, with masses of grip from its four-wheel drive system, make mincemeat of almost any supercar on a twisty back road. Be afraid of the Impreza Cosworth. It isn't a nice family hatchback.

 Power: *400bhp*

 0-60mph: *3.7 seconds*

 Top speed: *155mph*

 Price: *£50,000*

 Mad rating:

87

Subaru Impreza
Cosworth

Rover
Jet 1

Many aeroplanes use gas turbines, powerful engines that spin at huge speeds to generate enough huge amounts of energy. Immediately after the Second World War, British company Rover decided it would be a good idea to try and use a gas turbine to power a car.

It wasn't. By the standards of the day, the Jet 1 wasn't too slow – it could get to 60mph in about fourteen seconds, and manage over 90mph – but its fast-spinning turbine, which could revolve as many as 50,000 times every minute, was thirsty and very unreliable. Rover even entered a jet-powered car in the 24 Hours of Le Mans in 1963. It didn't finish the race.

Power: *140bhp*

0-60mph: *14 seconds*

Top speed: *90mph*

Price: *N/A*

Mad rating: 😈😈😈😈😈

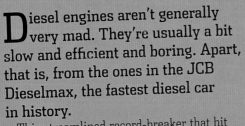

Diesel engines aren't generally very mad. They're usually a bit slow and efficient and boring. Apart, that is, from the ones in the JCB Dieselmax, the fastest diesel car in history.

This streamlined record-breaker that hit exactly 350mph in 2006, was driven by Andy Green, the same man who broke the land speed record in the Thrust SSC in 1997. The Dieselmax is powered by a pair of JCB turbodiesels, each of which puts out 750bhp – meaning a total power output of 1500bhp! Diesels? Boring? Not a bit of it...

 Power: 1500bhp

 0-60mph: N/A

 Top speed: 350mph

 Price: N/A

 Mad rating: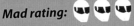

corus RICARDO   www.jcbdieselmax.com

JCB Dieselmax

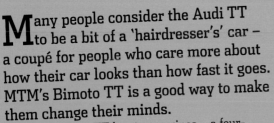

Many people consider the Audi TT to be a bit of a 'hairdresser's' car – a coupé for people who care more about how their car looks than how fast it goes. MTM's Bimoto TT is a good way to make them change their minds.

This tuned-up TT has two engines – a four-cylinder turbo at the front, and another in the boot – that combine to make a nice round 1000bhp. This makes MTM's TT the fastest tuned car in the world: in 2007, it recorded a dizzying 236mph on the Nardo high-speed circuit in Italy. Anyone still think it's a hairdresser's car?

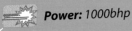 **Power:** 1000bhp

 0-60mph: 3.4 seconds

Top speed: 236mph

 Price: £600,000

 Mad rating: 👹👹👹👹

MTM Bimoto

Audi TT

Aston Martin makes some of the most beautiful-looking, beautiful-sounding, beautiful-driving cars in the world. So you'd expect Aston's own version of the Toyota iQ – the three-seater city car that James tested out in the boys' 'cheap and cheerful cars' challenge in 2009 – to have a big engine and lots more speed, right?

You'd be wrong. The Cygnet has the same engine as the normal iQ, so it'll still be depressingly slow. But much more expensive: the Aston costs twice as much as the Toyota equivalent. It's mad... in a bad way.

 Power: *100bhp approx*

 0-60mph: *11 seconds approx*

 Top speed: *100mph approx*

 Price: *£30,000 approx*

 Mad rating:

91

Aston Martin
Cygnet

Ahh, isn't the IndiGo all cute?

Look at it, all tiny and friendly faced and stubby... surely it couldn't hurt a fly? Yes, it could.

The IndiGo might look harmless, but behind those two seats lurks a giant V12 engine – the same one found in the Aston Martin DB9. Inspired by American IndyCar racers, this tiny-but-deadly roadster will buzz to 60mph in fewer than four seconds and onto a top speed of more than 170mph – at which point it will probably have hurt an awful lot of flies, as they're splattered all over the tiny windscreen. Don't be fooled: looks can be deceiving.

 Power: *435bhp*

 0-60mph: *3.9 seconds*

 Top speed: *171mph*

 Price: *N/A*

 Mad rating:

Ford IndiGo

92

191

93

Citroën
DS

Nowadays, Citroën makes grown-up, sane cars. But, back in the 1950s, the French company was a bit bonkers. The DS – a big, luxury car introduced in 1955 – was its maddest creation ever.

It had a fibreglass roof, suspension that magically levelled itself out, headlights that swivelled in the direction you steered... and a handbrake hidden down by the brake pedal. It didn't make much sense, but it was one of the most futuristic cars ever built. The French nicknamed it 'The Goddess', and the Citroën sold over 1.5 million DSs in the twenty years until 1975.

 Power: 60bhp

 0-60mph: 17.4 seconds

 Top speed: 93mph

 Price: £2,000

 Mad rating:

Most cars have one motor. Some have two. But the Jaguar C-X75 concept has... six. Does any car really need six motors? Jaguar thinks so.

This sleek, futuristic supercar has four electric motors – one in each wheel – which produce 780bhp. But there's more. The C-X75 also sports a pair of tiny jet turbines, which spin at a dizzying 80,000rpm (that's more than 1,300 revolutions every second!) to boost the power of the electric motors. Confused? So are we, but here's what it means: the C-X75 can do 0-60mph in 3.4 seconds and 205mph... but it's far less polluting than a Toyota Prius. Roll on the future of supercars!

 Power: *970bhp*

 0-60mph: *3.4 seconds*

 Top speed: *205mph*

 Price: *N/A*

 Mad rating: 🏁🏁🏁🏁

A lot of supercars use a bit of carbon fibre here and there. Lamborghini's Sesto Elemento concept is built completely of the stuff. That means it's very light, very strong and very, very expensive.

It's the same size as a Gallardo, but it weighs a huge 400kg less – that's the same as three sumo wrestlers! Which means that it's unbelievably quick off the line – 60mph comes up in just 2.5 seconds – and changes direction quicker than a mako shark. Oh, and it looks fantastically evil, too. As for the cost, well, Lamborghini won't reveal any numbers. But you can be sure they'd laugh in your face if you offered them less than a million pounds…

 Power: *570bhp*

 0-60mph: *2.5 seconds*

 Top speed: *More than 200mph*

 Price: *N/A*

 Mad rating:

Lamborghini
Sesto Elemento

If you could capture pure evil, then boil it down and turn it into a car, it would look like the Phantom Corsair.

This dark, frightening beast was created in California way back in 1938, and could manage 115mph, making it one of the fastest road cars in the world at the time. Under that long, sinister body was seating for six passengers – but finding five other people brave enough to get into the Corsair with you could prove a problem! Only one model was ever built, which is probably for the best. Is this the scariest-looking car that's ever existed?

 Power: 190bhp

 0-60mph: 12 seconds

 Top speed: 115mph

 Price: N/A

 Mad rating: 👾 👾 👾 👾

Phantom Corsair

'96

Maybach Exelero

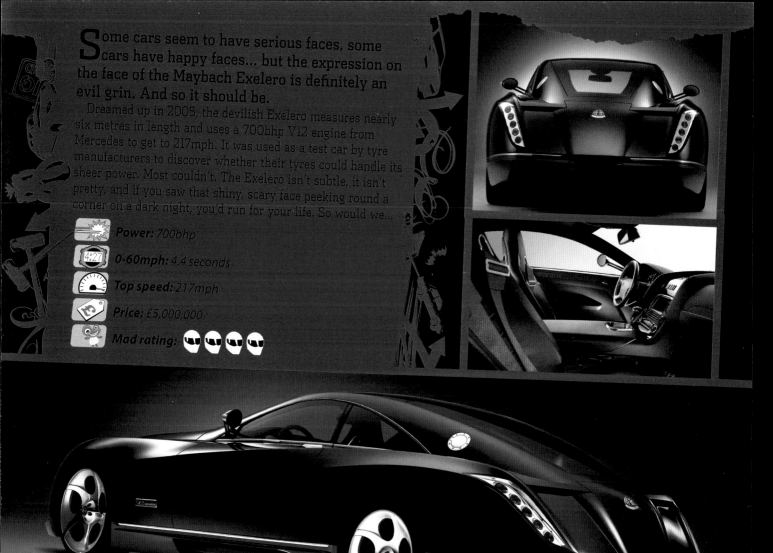

Some cars seem to have serious faces, some cars have happy faces... but the expression on the face of the Maybach Exelero is definitely an evil grin. And so it should be.

Dreamed up in 2005, the devilish Exelero measures nearly six metres in length and uses a 700bhp V12 engine from Mercedes to get to 217mph. It was used as a test car by tyre manufacturers to discover whether their tyres could handle its sheer power. Most couldn't. The Exelero isn't subtle, it isn't pretty, and if you saw that shiny, scary face peeking round a corner on a dark night, you'd run for your life. So would we...

Power: 700bhp

0-60mph: 4.4 seconds

Top speed: 217mph

Price: £5,000,000

Mad rating:

Remember the Caterham R500 that set a blistering time of 1m 17.9s around the *Top Gear* test track in 2008? Well, that thing looks like a boring old gold cart beside the Caterham Levante.

This speed machine has the same mechanicals as the R500 but, instead of a 263bhp Ford engine, it uses a 550bhp V8. That's twice the power, in a car that weighs the same. It'll rip to 60mph in fewer than three seconds and fling all but the best drivers into a hedge. Some cars are scary, some are terrifying... and then there's the Caterham Levante. Like a World War II bomb discovered after many years, this thing must be handled with care.

 Power: *550bhp*

 0-60mph: *2.9 seconds*

 Top speed: *150mph*

 Price: *£100,000*

 Mad rating: 😈😈😈😈😈

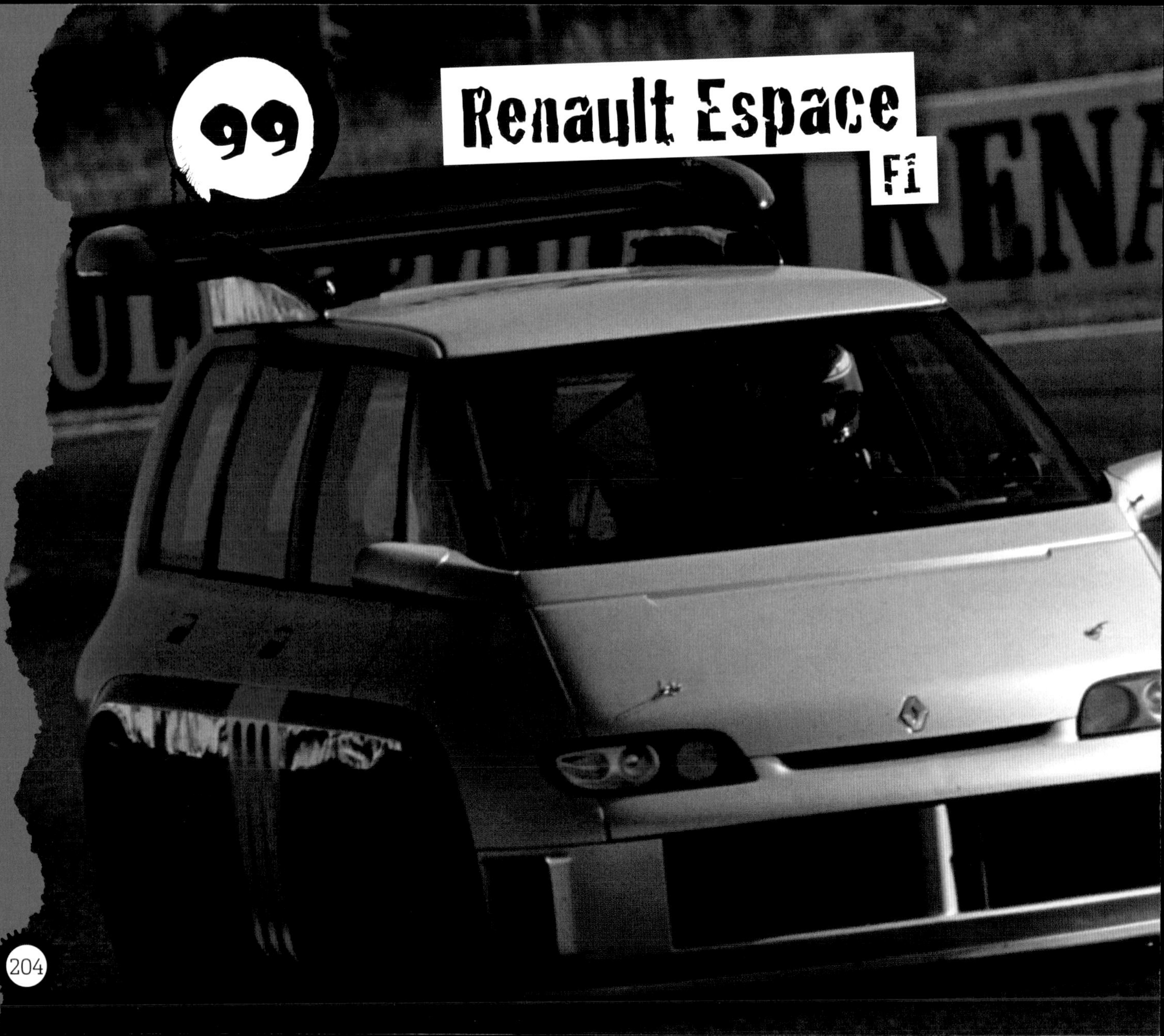

99 Renault Espace F1

If you've ever been stuck behind one on a narrow road, you'll know that big people carriers are far too slow. Thankfully Renault has the answer.

In 1995, French engineers fitted an Espace van with the 800bhp V10 engine from a Formula One car to make the fastest MPV in the world. The Espace F1 could get to 60mph in fewer than three seconds and had the absurd top speed of 194mph. If all parents drove these, no one would ever be late for school again. However, the Renault engineers did have to rip out all the rear seats to fit the engine in, so it might be a bit of a bumpy ride!

Power: *800bhp*

0-60mph: *Fewer than 3 seconds*

Top speed: *194mph*

Price: *N/A*

Mad rating:

Caparo T1

100

It isn't legal to drive a Formula One car on the road. There's a very good reason for this – within twenty seconds they'd be straight off the road and into the nearest ditch.

But the Caparo T1 was created to be the closest thing to an F1 car that was legal to drive on the road. It was very nearly as scary. 'If you try to go round a normal roundabout at a normal speed in this,' screamed Jeremy when he tested the T1 in 2007, 'You're going to have a huge accident!' But on the track, the T1 was brutally fast. It could hit 60mph in just two and a half seconds, and would accelerate all the way to 205mph... so long as it didn't catch fire first!

 Power: *575bhp*

 **0-60mph:** *2.5 seconds*

 Top speed: *205mph*

 **Price** *£235,000*

 Mad rating: